NKK PROSPECTUS : FINE ARTS

NRITYANGANA KALA KENDRA

Contents

Nrityangana Kala Kendra Fine Arts

Prospectus

Nrityangana Kala Kendra

Vaishali, Ghaziabad, Uttar Pradesh - 201010

CHAPTER ONE

About Nrityangana Kala Kendra

Introduction

Nrityangana Kala Kendra (OPC) Private Limited or NKK was established by Swarnika in 2021. The company has been incorporated with the Government of India under the section 8 of the Companies Act, 2013. The company has been registered with ISO 9001:2015 (International Organization for Standardization) and IAF (International Accreditation Forum) with EGAC (Egyptian Accreditation Council). The courses meet the international standards and have been modelled on the given guidelines.

Objectives

The company has been established with the following objectives in mind-

- To facilitate valid certification of the various forms of art in India.

- To facilitate valid certification of the various forms of art as per the international standards.
- To facilitate affordable skill enhancement education.
- To facilitate affordable knowledge-based education.
- To facilitate affordable hobby-inclined education.
- To facilitate efficient and effective entrance preparation.
- To facilitate affordable entrance preparation.
- To facilitate flexibility while pursuing programs.
- To provide online and doorstep education to the learners.
- To promote and develop distance education in India.

Prominent Features

NKK has these unique features-

- Registered with the Government of India
- Registered with ISO and IAF with EGAC
- Affordable and cost-effective courses
- Online and Doorstep Education
- Flexible Admission Rules
- Individualised Study (flexibility in the place, pace, and duration of study)
- Flexible Study Hours
- Use of latest information and communication technologies
- Modular and sectional programs
- Socially and academically relevant programs based on the learner's needs

Academic Programs

The company offers both short-term and long-term programs leading to Certificates and Diplomas, covering conventional as well as innovative programs in the field of Arts and Humanities. Some programs are focused solely on the preparation of entrances (like UGC-NET, CUCET, CUET, etc). The certificates and diplomas measure up to international standards.

Instructional Mode

The company provides a multi-media approach in imparting instructions to its learners. It includes the following-

- Printed course material (can be purchased at the time of admission or later online)
- Electronic course material (can be purchased at the time of admission or later online)
- Assignments for assessment and feedback
- Tests for assessment and feedback
- Practice Tests for self-assessment
- Supporting audio-visual material
- Live interactions
- Project work in some programs
- Online Examination and Submission

Credit System

Nrityangana Kala Kendra follows the 'Credit System' for most of its programs. Each credit in our system amounts to 20 hours of study comprising of all learning activities. The hours of study have been referred to as 'credit hours' as they result in earning the credits. Thus, a 3 credit program would involve 60 credit hours. This helps the learner to understand the academic effort one has to put in, in order to successfully complete a course. Completion of an academic program (Certificate or Diploma) requires successful clearance of both the assignments and the examinations of each course in a program.

Evaluation System

Nrityangana Kala Kendra follows a unique evaluation system-

- Self-assessment exercises
- Self-assessment practice tests
- Continuous evaluation through assignments and feedback
- Continuous evaluation through tests and feedback
- Seminars and workshops
- Project work
- Term-end assignment
- Term-end examination

The evaluation of learners depends upon various instructional activities undertaken by them. All the assignments and tests are mandatory and should be completed in time. The weightage of marks would differ from program to program and would be mentioned in the course outline.

NKK adopts both score-based and grade-based methods of evaluation for learners' performance. The score correlates of the letter grades are as follows-

Grading System: (percentage)	
O	91-100
A+	81-90
A	71-80
B+	61-70
B	51-60
C	40-50
F	Below 40

The students have to maintain a 40% minimum score throughout the program. The final result would also show the division achieved.

Division chart:-

More than or equal to 40 but less than 50
THIRD DIVISION

More than or equal to 50 but less than 60'
SECOND DIVISION

More than or equal to 60 but less than 75
FIRST DIVISION

More than or equal to 75 but less than 90
FIRST DIVISION WITH DISTINCTION

90 and above
FIRST DIVISION WITH HONORS

Rules and Regulation

- No malpractices adopted while taking tests, assignments, and examinations would be tolerated.
- Unpleasant behavior towards the company, teaching staff, non-teaching staff, or other learners would not be tolerated.
- Once paid, the fees would not be refunded until and unless the course is canceled by the company itself for the session.
- Everyone is treated equally.
- Change of elective is allowed once for diploma programs within 3 months of commencement of program session. The student has to make a payment of Rs. 300 per course for this.

- For any change of elective, address, and other information, write to swara@nrityanganakalakendra.com.
- Assignments and examinations are to be completed by the allotted due date. The program needs to be completed before the provided deadline.
- Incomplete and late application forms/ re-registration forms, wrong options of courses or electives in diploma programs, incorrect or false information will be rejected without any intimation to the learners. the learners are, therefore, advised to fill the relevant columns carefully and enclose all the attested copies of the necessary documents asked for, and submit the form before the due date.
- Learners can be simultaneously enrolled in two diploma programs while pursuing a degree program with any university. Enrollment in more than two diploma courses is prohibited in a single academic year. One certificate course can be opted for along with two diploma courses. Up to three certificate courses can be taken up at a time along with one diploma course. In case of no diploma courses being opted for, a student can take up to four certificate courses at a time.
- Learners don't have to visit the centre at any time. All information would be communicated online. Deliverables would be dispatched to their registered address.

CHAPTER TWO

Fine Arts

The level clearance program has been modeled after international standards. The sectional modules can be taken up online or at registered academies or schools. There is an introductory certificate program followed by level programs. There are five levels with two parts each-

1. Certificate: Basics of Fine Arts (CBFA) : 6 months - 1 year

2. Fine Arts Level 1 Part A (FAL1A) : 3 months - 1 year

3. Fine Arts Level 1 Part B (FAL1B) : 3 months - 1 year

4. Fine Arts Level 2 Part A (FAL2A) : 3 months - 1 year

5. Fine Arts Level 2 Part B (FAL2B) : 3 months - 1 year

6. Fine Arts Level 3 Part A (FAL3A) : 6 months - 1 year

7. Fine Arts Level 3 Part B (FAL3B) : 6 months - 1 year

8. Fine Arts Level 4 Part A (FAL4A) : 6 months - 1 year

9. Fine Arts Level 4 Part B (FAL4B) : 6 months - 1 year

10. Fine Arts Level 5 {with Presentation} (FAL5) : 1 year - 2 years

11. Post-Graduate Diploma in Fine Arts (PGDFA) : 1 year - 3 years

CHAPTER THREE

Certificate: Basics of Fine Arts

Course Code: CBFA

Eligibility: Anyone can take up this course.

Minimum Duration: 6 months

Maximum Duration: 1 year

*If the learner hasn't completed the course by the end of the given time period, they'll have to re-register to continue.

Fees: Program Fees including Registration Fees Rs. 2000

*Fees after Promotional Discount is Rs. 1500.

*Re-registration fees Rs. 200 for each year.

Academic Sessions: Flexible Commencement (Validity of 1 year from the date of enrollment)

Examination Sessions: March, June, September, December

*Learner needs to re-register after four examination sessions have been passed. Also, if a learner gives the examination in a particular session and fails to obtain the minimum marks, they can re-take the examination in the next session (within the four sessions of the enrollment year) for an additional amount of Rs. 200.

*The detailed form is included at the beginning of the purchased course. Once purchased, no amount will be refunded.

*Any malpractice or misconduct from the learner's end would not be tolerated.

Course Coordinator: Prof. Swarnika (swara@nrityanganakalakendra.com)

Syllabus:-

- Art- theory, elements, principles, concept
- Freehand drawing
- Colours- concept, types, perception of colours in nature, and colour wheel
- Geometrical shapes
- Still Life- Drawing, Shading, Painting
- Drawing simple forms, floral art, and natural shapes
- drawing through geometrical shapes
- Designs- geometrical and floral
- Vegetable printing and Hand printing (thumb and finger impressions)
- Importance of art in everyday life
- Patterns and textures
- Eye-level and horizon (with usage)
- Foreground, Middle-ground, and Background
- Typography
- Aesthetics

Credit Hours: 60 hours

Credits: 3

Material: The electronic study material has been included in the online course. Relevant audios and videos would be added to the course outlay for practice. There will be 10 live sessions scheduled.

*Additional Material that could be taken is "Theorization of Fine Arts: Part A and B" (Swarnika).

Evaluation:- Term-end evaluation (conducted online)

- Theory- 20%
- Practical- 70%
- Assignment- 10%

*A minimum score of 40% has to be maintained throughout the examination.

Division chart:-

More than or equal to 40 but less than 50
THIRD DIVISION

More than or equal to 50 but less than 60
SECOND DIVISION

More than or equal to 60 but less than 75
FIRST DIVISION

More than or equal to 75 but less than 90
FIRST DIVISION WITH DISTINCTION

90 and above
FIRST DIVISION WITH HONORS

Grading System: (percentage)	
O	91-100
A+	81-90
A	71-80
B+	61-70
B	51-60
C	40-50
F	Below 40

CHAPTER FOUR

Fine Arts Level 1 Part A

Course Code: FAL1A

Eligibility: Completion of Certificate: Basics of Fine Arts (CBFA) or equivalent course with 80 credit hours.

Minimum Duration: 3 months

Maximum Duration: 1 year

*If the learner hasn't completed the course by the end of the given time period, they'll have to re-register to continue.

Registration Fees: Rs. 1500

*Fees after Promotional Discount is Rs. 1200

*Re-registration fees for examination - Rs. 500

Program Fees: Rs. 3000

*Fees after Promotional Discount is Rs. 2500

Registration and Program Fees: Rs. 4500

*Fees after Promotional Discount is Rs. 3500

Academic Sessions: Flexible Commencement (Validity of 1 year from the date of enrollment)

Examination Sessions: March, June, September, December

*Learner needs to re-register after four examination sessions have been passed. Also, if a learner gives the

examination in a particular session and fails to obtain the minimum marks, they can re-take the examination in the next session (within the four sessions of the enrollment year) for an additional amount of Rs. 500.

*Once purchased, no amount will be refunded.

*Any malpractice or misconduct from the learner's end would not be tolerated.

Course Coordinator: Prof. Swarnika (swara@nrityanganakalakendra.com)

<u>Syllabus:-</u>

The syllabus has been divided into three modules-

<u>FAL1A Module 1</u>

- Theory of Art
- Importance of Art
- Elements of Art
- Principles of Art
- Types of Colours
- Perception of Colours in Nature
- Lines
- Balance
- Forms of Art
- Textures
- Patterns and textures
- Eye level and its use in painting
- Horizon and its use in painting
- Colour Wheel
- Aesthetics

15 credit hours

<u>FAL1A Module 2</u>

- Still Life Painting
- Still Life Pencil Shading
- Drawing simple forms
- Drawing floral art
- Drawing natural objects
- Geometrical designs
- Floral designs
- Picture Composition
- Pencil Shading Composition
- Typography

50 credit hours

FAL1A Module 3

- Art of Prehistoric Period
- Indus Valley Civilization
- History and Appreciation of Art

15 credit hours

Submission

- Essay assignment from Module 1
- Essay assignment from Module 3
- Still Life Painting- Water Colours
- Still Life Pencil Shading
- Still Life Pencil Colour Shading
- Drawing and colouring of five simple forms
- Drawing and colouring of five floral art
- Drawing and colouring of five natural objects
- Two geometrical designs
- Two floral designs

- Water Colour/Oil Pastel Picture Composition
- Pencil Shading Picture Composition
- Two Typography designs
- Colour Wheel

Total Credit Hours: 80 hours

Total Credits: 4

Material: The hardcopy of the study material (of all modules) could be availed from Nrityangana Kala Kendra for an additional amount of Rs. 400. The learners could also buy the study material online. The electronic copy could be purchased from kindle. The relevant links will be shared in the course. You can also write an email to swara@nrityanganakalakendra.com for any queries. Video and audio recordings will be available to students who sign up for the online program. There will be 10 live classes.

Evaluation:- Term-end evaluation (conducted online)

- Theory- 10%
- Practical- 40%
- Assignments and Submissions- 50%

Grading System: (percentage)

O	91-100
A+	81-90
A	71-80
B+	61-70
B	51-60
C	40-50
F	Below 40

Division chart:-

More than or equal to 40 but less than 50
THIRD DIVISION

More than or equal to 50 but less than 60
SECOND DIVISION

More than or equal to 60 but less than 75
FIRST DIVISION

More than or equal to 75 but less than 90
FIRST DIVISION WITH DISTINCTION

90 and above
FIRST DIVISION WITH HONORS

CHAPTER FIVE

Fine Arts Level 1 Part B

Course Code: FAL1B

Eligibility: Successful completion of FAL1A

Minimum Duration: 3 months

Maximum Duration: 1 year

*If the learner hasn't completed the course by the end of the given time period, they'll have to re-register to continue.

Registration Fees: Rs. 1500

*Fees after Promotional Discount is Rs. 1200

*Re-registration fees for examination - Rs. 500

Program Fees: Rs. 3000

*Fees after Promotional Discount is Rs. 2500

Registration and Program Fees: Rs. 4500

*Fees after Promotional Discount is Rs. 3500

Academic Sessions: Flexible Commencement (Validity of 1 year from the date of enrollment)

Examination Sessions: March, June, September, December

*Learner needs to re-register after four examination sessions have been passed. Also, if a learner gives the examination in a particular session and fails to obtain the

minimum marks, they can re-take the examination in the next session (within the four sessions of the enrollment year) for an additional amount of Rs. 500.

*Once purchased, no amount will be refunded.

*Any malpractice or misconduct from the learner's end would not be tolerated.

Course Coordinator: Prof. Swarnika (swara@nrityanganakalakendra.com)

Syllabus:-

The syllabus has been divided into three modules-

<u>FAL1B Module 1</u>

- Vanishing Points
- Foreground
- Middle-ground
- Background
- Nature of Colours
- Illustrations

10 credit hours

<u>FAL1B Module 2</u>

- Pastel Shading
- Pastel Colouring
- Natural Landscape
- Texture Colouring
- Illustrations
- Picture Composition
- Mandal Art Designs

50 credit hours

FAL1B Module 3

- Art from Mauryan Period
- Art from Sunga Period
- Art from Kushan Period
- Art from Gandhar Period
- Patna School of Art

20 credit hours

Submission

- Essay assignment from Module 1
- Essay assignment from Module 3
- Pastel Shading
- Pastel Colouring
- Two Natural Landscaping
- Five Texture Colouring
- Two Illustrations
- Picture Composition
- Two Mandal Art Designs

Total Credit Hours: 80 hours
Total Credits: 4
Material: The hardcopy of the study material (of all modules) could be availed from Nrityangana Kala Kendra for an additional amount of Rs. 400. The learners could also buy the study material online. The electronic copy could be purchased from kindle. The relevant links will be shared in the course. You can also write an email to swara@nrityanganakalakendra.com for any queries. Video and audio recordings will be available to students who sign up for the online program. There will be 10 live classes.

Evaluation:- Term-end evaluation (conducted online)

- Theory- 10%
- Practical- 40%
- Assignments and Submissions- 50%

Grading System: (percentage)	
O	91-100
A+	81-90
A	71-80
B+	61-70
B	51-60
C	40-50
F	Below 40

Division chart:-

More than or equal to 40 but less than 50
THIRD DIVISION

More than or equal to 50 but less than 60
SECOND DIVISION

More than or equal to 60 but less than 75
FIRST DIVISION

More than or equal to 75 but less than 90
FIRST DIVISION WITH DISTINCTION

90 and above
FIRST DIVISION WITH HONORS

CHAPTER SIX

Fine Arts Level 2 Part A

Course Code: FAL2A

Eligibility: Successful completion of FAL1B

Minimum Duration: 3 months

Maximum Duration: 1 year

*If the learner hasn't completed the course by the end of the given time period, they'll have to re-register to continue.

Registration Fees: Rs. 1500

*Fees after Promotional Discount is Rs. 1200

*Re-registration fees for examination - Rs. 500

Program Fees: Rs. 4000

*Fees after Promotional Discount is Rs. 3500

Registration and Program Fees: Rs. 5500

*Fees after Promotional Discount is Rs. 4500

Academic Sessions: Flexible Commencement (Validity of 1 year from the date of enrollment)

Examination Sessions: March, June, September, December

*Learner needs to re-register after four examination sessions have been passed. Also, if a learner gives the examination in a particular session and fails to obtain the

minimum marks, they can re-take the examination in the next session (within the four sessions of the enrollment year) for an additional amount of Rs. 500.

*Once purchased, no amount will be refunded.

*Any malpractice or misconduct from the learner's end would not be tolerated.

Course Coordinator: Prof. Swarnika (swara@nrityanganakalakendra.com)

<u>Syllabus:-</u>

The syllabus has been divided into three modules-

<u>FAL2A Module 1</u>

- Force
- Rhythm
- Mass Volume and Proportion
- Freehand and line drawing
- Scope of Art
- Light and Dark Solidity

5 credit hours

<u>FAL2A Module 2</u>

- Freehand Drawing
- Line Drawing
- Nature Study
- Light and Dark Solidity
- Mass Volume and Proportion
- Ornamental Designs
- Geometrical Designs
- Shringar Rasa Depictive Painting

40 credit hours

FAL2A Module 3

- Art from Gupta Period
- Cave Paintings- Ajanta, Bagh, Sittanvassal, Badami, Ellora-Ellephanta, etc.
- Jain School of Paintings
- Rajasthani Paintings
- History of Indian Art
- Illustrations

10 credit hours

FAL2A Module 4

- Pablo Picasso
- Vincent Van Gogh
- Leonardo Da Vinci

5 credit hours

FAL2A Module 5

- Neolithic Cultures: Native American Neolithic Cultures

20 credit hours

Submission

- Essay on Module 1
- Essay on Module 3
- Essay on Module 4
- Assignment on Module 5

- Freehand Drawing
- Line Drawing
- Nature Study
- Light and Dark Solidity
- Mass Volume and Proportion
- Two Ornamental Designs
- Two Geometrical Designs
- Shringar Rasa Depictive Series

Total Credit Hours: 80 hours
Total Credits: 4
Material: The hardcopy of the study material (of all modules) could be availed from Nrityangana Kala Kendra for an additional amount of Rs. 500. The learners could also buy the study material online. The electronic copy could be purchased from kindle. The relevant links will be shared in the course. You can also write an email to swara@nrityanganakalakendra.com for any queries. Video and audio recordings will be available to students who sign up for the online program. There will be 10 live classes.

Evaluation:- Term-end evaluation (conducted online)

- Theory- 10%
- Practical- 40%
- Assignments and Submissions- 50%

Grading System: (percentage)	
O	91-100
A+	81-90
A	71-80
B+	61-70
B	51-60
C	40-50
F	Below 40

Division chart:-

More than or equal to 40 but less than 50
THIRD DIVISION

More than or equal to 50 but less than 60
SECOND DIVISION

More than or equal to 60 but less than 75
FIRST DIVISION

More than or equal to 75 but less than 90
FIRST DIVISION WITH DISTINCTION

90 and above
FIRST DIVISION WITH HONORS

CHAPTER SEVEN

Fine Arts Level 2 Part B

Course Code: FAL2B

Eligibility: Successful completion of FAL2A

Minimum Duration: 3 months

Maximum Duration: 1 year

*If the learner hasn't completed the course by the end of the given time period, they'll have to re-register to continue.

Registration Fees: Rs. 1500

*Fees after Promotional Discount is Rs. 1200

*Re-registration fees for examination - Rs. 500

Program Fees: Rs. 4000

*Fees after Promotional Discount is Rs. 3500

Registration and Program Fees: Rs. 5500

*Fees after Promotional Discount is Rs. 4500

Academic Sessions: Flexible Commencement (Validity of 1 year from the date of enrollment)

Examination Sessions: March, June, September, December

*Learner needs to re-register after four examination sessions have been passed. Also, if a learner gives the examination in a particular session and fails to obtain the

minimum marks, they can re-take the examination in the next session (within the four sessions of the enrollment year) for an additional amount of Rs. 500.

*Once purchased, no amount will be refunded.

*Any malpractice or misconduct from the learner's end would not be tolerated.

Course Coordinator: Prof. Swarnika (swara@nrityanganakalakendra.com)

<u>**Syllabus:-**</u>

The syllabus has been divided into three modules-

<u>FAL2B Module 1</u>

- Perspective
- Intuition
- Beauty
- Religion
- Morality
- Sculpture
- Miniature
- Value
- Hue
- Intensity
- Tints
- Tones
- Shades
- Manuscripts
- Psychology of Colours

10 credit hours

<u>FAL2B Module 2</u>

- Perspective Landscape Drawing

- Perspective Still Life Drawing
- Mosaic Art
- Hasya Rasa Painting

30 credit hours

<u>FAL2B Module 3</u>

- Art of China
- Greek Art- Classical Period
- Greek Art- Hellenistic Period
- Roman Art
- Shadangas of Indian Art
- Pahadi School of Art
- Origin of Indian Sculptures

15 credit hours

<u>FAL2B Module 4</u>

- Michelangelo
- M. F. Husain
- Claude Monet

5 credit hours

<u>FAL2B Module 5</u>

- Prehistoric Turkey and Historic Mesopotamia

20 credit hours

<u>Submission</u>

- Essay on Module 1
- Essay on Module 3
- Essay on Module 4
- Assignment on Module 5
- Two Perspective Landscape Drawing
- Two Perspective Still Life Drawing
- Two Mosaic Art
- Hasya Rasa Series

Total Credit Hours: 80 hours

Total Credits: 4

Material: The hardcopy of the study material (of all modules) could be availed from Nrityangana Kala Kendra for an additional amount of Rs. 500. The learners could also buy the study material online. The electronic copy could be purchased from kindle. The relevant links will be shared in the course. You can also write an email to swara@nrityanganakalakendra.com for any queries. Video and audio recordings will be available to students who sign up for the online program. There will be 10 live classes.

Evaluation:- Term-end evaluation (conducted online)

- Theory- 10%
- Practical- 40%
- Assignments and Submissions- 50%

Grading System: (percentage)	
O	91-100
A+	81-90
A	71-80
B+	61-70
B	51-60
C	40-50
F	Below 40

Division chart:-

More than or equal to 40 but less than 50
THIRD DIVISION

More than or equal to 50 but less than 60
SECOND DIVISION

More than or equal to 60 but less than 75
FIRST DIVISION

More than or equal to 75 but less than 90
FIRST DIVISION WITH DISTINCTION

90 and above
FIRST DIVISION WITH HONORS

CHAPTER EIGHT

Fine Arts Level 3 Part A

Course Code: FAL3A

Eligibility: Successful completion of FAL2B

Minimum Duration: 6 months

Maximum Duration: 1 year

*If the learner hasn't completed the course by the end of the given time period, they'll have to re-register to continue.

Registration Fees: Rs. 2000

*Fees after Promotional Discount is Rs. 1500

*Re-registration fees for examination - Rs. 500

Program Fees: Rs. 3500

*Fees after Promotional Discount is Rs. 3200

Registration and Program Fees: Rs. 5500

*Fees after Promotional Discount is Rs. 4500

Academic Sessions: Flexible Commencement (Validity of 1 year from the date of enrollment)

Examination Sessions: March, June, September, December

*Learner needs to re-register after four examination sessions have been passed. Also, if a learner gives the examination in a particular session and fails to obtain the

minimum marks, they can re-take the examination in the next session (within the four sessions of the enrollment year) for an additional amount of Rs. 500.

*Once purchased, no amount will be refunded.

*Any malpractice or misconduct from the learner's end would not be tolerated.

Course Coordinator: Prof. Swarnika (swara@nrityanganakalakendra.com)

<u>Syllabus:-</u>

The syllabus has been divided into three modules-

<u>FAL3A Module 1</u>

- Theories of Creativity and Rasas
- Application of Rasas in Art
- Indian Aesthetics

20 credit hours

<u>FAL3A Module 2</u>

- Geometrical Designs using Ratio and Proportion
- Floral Designs using Ratio and Proportion
- Sketching Nature Art
- Colouring Nature Art
- Poster Making
- Karuna Rasa Painting

50 credit hours

<u>FAL3A Module 3</u>

- Art from Mughal Period
- Sculptures from Mohan Jodaro and Harappa

- Mauryan period Sculptures

20 credit hours

<u>FAL3A Module 4</u>

- Edouard Manet
- Pierre-Auguste-Renoir
- Edgar Degas

10 credit hours

<u>FAL3A Module 5</u>

- Neolithic China and the Early Dynasties

20 credit hours

<u>Submission</u>

- Essay on Module 1
- Essay on Module 3
- Essay on Module 4
- Assignment on Module 5
- Two Geometrical Designs using Ratio and Proportion
- Two Floral Designs using Ratio and Proportion
- Sketching Nature Art
- Watercolour Nature Art
- Acrylic Colour Nature Art
- Three Posters
- Karuna Rasa Series

Total Credit Hours: 120 hours

Total Credits: 6

Material: The hardcopy of the study material (of all modules) could be availed from Nrityangana Kala Kendra for an additional amount of Rs. 800. The learners could also buy the study material online. The electronic copy could be purchased from kindle. The relevant links will be shared in the course. You can also write an email to swara@nrityanganakalakendra.com for any queries. Video and audio recordings will be available to students who sign up for the online program. There will be 15 live classes.

Evaluation:- Term-end evaluation (conducted online)

- Theory- 10%
- Practical- 40%
- Assignments and Submissions- 50%

Grading System: (percentage)	
O	91-100
A+	81-90
A	71-80
B+	61-70
B	51-60
C	40-50
F	Below 40

Division chart:-

More than or equal to 40 but less than 50
THIRD DIVISION

More than or equal to 50 but less than 60
SECOND DIVISION

More than or equal to 60 but less than 75
FIRST DIVISION

More than or equal to 75 but less than 90
FIRST DIVISION WITH DISTINCTION

90 and above
FIRST DIVISION WITH HONORS

CHAPTER NINE

Fine Arts Level 3 Part B

Course Code: FAL3B

Eligibility: Successful completion of FAL3A

Minimum Duration: 6 months

Maximum Duration: 1 year

*If the learner hasn't completed the course by the end of the given time period, they'll have to re-register to continue.

Registration Fees: Rs. 2000

*Fees after Promotional Discount is Rs. 1500

*Re-registration fees for examination - Rs. 500

Program Fees: Rs. 3500

*Fees after Promotional Discount is Rs. 3200

Registration and Program Fees: Rs. 5500

*Fees after Promotional Discount is Rs. 4500

Academic Sessions: Flexible Commencement (Validity of 1 year from the date of enrollment)

Examination Sessions: March, June, September, December

*Learner needs to re-register after four examination sessions have been passed. Also, if a learner gives the examination in a particular session and fails to obtain the

minimum marks, they can re-take the examination in the next session (within the four sessions of the enrollment year) for an additional amount of Rs. 500.

*Once purchased, no amount will be refunded.

*Any malpractice or misconduct from the learner's end would not be tolerated.

Course Coordinator: Prof. Swarnika (swara@nrityanganakalakendra.com)

Syllabus:-

The syllabus has been divided into three modules-

FAL3B Module 1

- Comparison between Indian and Western Styles of Figures (drawing)
- Difference between Modern and Abstract Art
- Modern Art
- Difference between Western Art and Modern Art

10 credit hours

FAL3B Module 2

- On the spot Landscaping (water and poster)
- Modern Art
- Life Study (pencil)
- Book Covers
- Raudra Rasa Painting

50 credit hours

FAL3B Module 3

- Early Christian and Byzantine Art

- Renaissance in Italy
- Kal Pasutra Manuscripts
- Architecture of Mughal Period

20 credit hours

<u>FAL3B Module 4</u>

- Paul Cezanne
- Berthe Morlsot
- Mary Cassatt

20 credit hours

<u>FAL3B Module 5</u>

- Egyptian Art

20 credit hours

<u>Submission</u>

- Essay on Module 1
- Essay on Module 3
- Essay on Module 4
- Assignment on Module 5
- On the spot Landscaping (water)
- On the spot Landscaping (poster)
- Two pieces of Modern Art
- Two Life Study (pencil)
- Two Book Covers
- Raudra Rasa Series

Total Credit Hours: 120 hours

Total Credits: 6

Material: The hardcopy of the study material (of all modules) could be availed from Nrityangana Kala Kendra for an additional amount of Rs. 800. The learners could also buy the study material online. The electronic copy could be purchased from kindle. The relevant links will be shared in the course. You can also write an email to swara@nrityanganakalakendra.com for any queries. Video and audio recordings will be available to students who sign up for the online program. There will be 15 live classes.

Evaluation:- Term-end evaluation (conducted online)

- Theory- 10%
- Practical- 40%
- Assignments and Submissions- 50%

Grading System: (percentage)	
O	91-100
A+	81-90
A	71-80
B+	61-70
B	51-60
C	40-50
F	Below 40

Division chart:-

More than or equal to 40 but less than 50
THIRD DIVISION

More than or equal to 50 but less than 60
SECOND DIVISION

More than or equal to 60 but less than 75
FIRST DIVISION

More than or equal to 75 but less than 90
FIRST DIVISION WITH DISTINCTION

90 and above
FIRST DIVISION WITH HONORS

CHAPTER TEN

Fine Arts Level 4 Part A

Course Code: FAL4A

Eligibility: Successful completion of FAL3B

Minimum Duration: 6 months

Maximum Duration: 1 year

*If the learner hasn't completed the course by the end of the given time period, they'll have to re-register to continue.

Registration Fees: Rs. 2000

*Fees after Promotional Discount is Rs. 1500

*Re-registration fees for examination - Rs. 500

Program Fees: Rs. 4000

*Fees after Promotional Discount is Rs. 3700

Registration and Program Fees: Rs. 6000

*Fees after Promotional Discount is Rs. 5000

Academic Sessions: Flexible Commencement (Validity of 1 year from the date of enrollment)

Examination Sessions: March, June, September, December

*Learner needs to re-register after four examination sessions have been passed. Also, if a learner gives the examination in a particular session and fails to obtain the

minimum marks, they can re-take the examination in the next session (within the four sessions of the enrollment year) for an additional amount of Rs. 500.

*Once purchased, no amount will be refunded.

*Any malpractice or misconduct from the learner's end would not be tolerated.

Course Coordinator: Prof. Swarnika (swara@nrityanganakalakendra.com)

<u>**Syllabus:-**</u>

The syllabus has been divided into three modules-

<u>FAL4A Module 1</u>

- Abstract Art
- Folk Art
- Indian Folk Art
- Antique Study and Antique Art

20 credit hours

<u>FAL4A Module 2</u>

- Abstract Art
- Folk Art
- Antique Study (pencil)
- Veera Rasa SeriesOverall Designs
- Composition Painting (Acrylic and Oil)
- Veera Rasa painting

50 credit hours

<u>FAL4A Module 3</u>

- Didarganj Yakshi, Amravati Yakshas and Yakshinis

- Sanchi Stupas
- Post-impressionism
- Artists of 18th Century

20 credit hours

FAL4A Module 4

- Rococco
- Chardin
- Hograth
- Blake
- Gainsborough

10 credit hours

FAL4A Module 5

- Aegean Art and the Cyclades
- Art of Greece
- Art of Rome

20 credit hours

Submission

- Essay on Module 1
- Essay on Module 3
- Essay on Module 4
- Assignment on Module 5
- Two works of Abstract Art
- Five different kinds of Folk Art
- Two works from Antique Study (pencil)

- Five dfferent kinds of Designs
- Acrylic Colour Composition Painting
- Composition Oil Painting
- Veera Rasa Series

Total Credit Hours: 120 hours
Total Credits: 6
Material: The hardcopy of the study material (of all modules) could be availed from Nrityangana Kala Kendra for an additional amount of Rs. 800. The learners could also buy the study material online. The electronic copy could be purchased from kindle. The relevant links will be shared in the course. You can also write an email to swara@nrityanganakalakendra.com for any queries. Video and audio recordings will be available to students who sign up for the online program. There will be 15 live classes.

Evaluation:- Term-end evaluation (conducted online)

- Theory- 10%
- Practical- 40%
- Assignments and Submissions- 50%

Grading System: (percentage)	
O	91-100
A+	81-90
A	71-80
B+	61-70
B	51-60
C	40-50
F	Below 40

Division chart:-

More than or equal to 40 but less than 50
THIRD DIVISION

More than or equal to 50 but less than 60
SECOND DIVISION

More than or equal to 60 but less than 75
FIRST DIVISION

More than or equal to 75 but less than 90
FIRST DIVISION WITH DISTINCTION

90 and above
FIRST DIVISION WITH HONORS

CHAPTER ELEVEN

Fine Arts Level 4 Part B

Course Code: FAL4B

Eligibility: Successful completion of FAL4A

Minimum Duration: 6 months

Maximum Duration: 1 year

*If the learner hasn't completed the course by the end of the given time period, they'll have to re-register to continue.

Registration Fees: Rs. 2000

*Fees after Promotional Discount is Rs. 1500

*Re-registration fees for examination - Rs. 500

Program Fees: Rs. 4000

*Fees after Promotional Discount is Rs. 3700

Registration and Program Fees: Rs. 6000

*Fees after Promotional Discount is Rs. 5000

Academic Sessions: Flexible Commencement (Validity of 1 year from the date of enrollment)

Examination Sessions: March, June, September, December

*Learner needs to re-register after four examination sessions have been passed. Also, if a learner gives the examination in a particular session and fails to obtain the

minimum marks, they can re-take the examination in the next session (within the four sessions of the enrollment year) for an additional amount of Rs. 500.

*Once purchased, no amount will be refunded.

*Any malpractice or misconduct from the learner's end would not be tolerated.

Course Coordinator: Prof. Swarnika (swara@nrityanganakalakendra.com)

Syllabus:-

The syllabus has been divided into three modules-

FAL4B Module 1

- Realistic Art
- Impressionism
- Impact of Persian Art over Indian Art
- Modernism
- Post-Modernism
- Evolution of Oil painting

10 credit hours

FAL4B Module 2

- Antique Study (charcoal)
- Charcoal Picture Composition
- Life Study Charcoal
- Still Life Charcoal
- Bhayanak Rasa Painting

30 credit hours

FAL4B Module 3

- Indian Sculptures- Mathura and Amravati School of Art
- Modern Art Movement
- Artists of the 17th Century

15 credit hours

<u>FAL4B Module 4</u>

- Poussin
- Rembrandt
- Varneer
- Franshals
- El-greco
- Berhani
- Michaelangelo

5 credit hours

<u>FAL4B Module 5</u>

- Romanesque and Gothic Art
- Art of Mesoamerica
- Early Christian, Byzantine and Islamic Art

20 credit hours

<u>Submission</u>

- Essay on Module 1
- Essay on Module 3
- Essay on Module 4
- Assignment on Module 5
- Two Antique Study (charcoal)

- Two Charcoal Picture Compositions
- Two Life Study Charcoal
- Two Still Life Charcoal
- Bhayanak Rasa Series

Total Credit Hours: 120 hours
Total Credits: 6
Material: The hardcopy of the study material (of all modules) could be availed from Nrityangana Kala Kendra for an additional amount of Rs. 800. The learners could also buy the study material online. The electronic copy could be purchased from kindle. The relevant links will be shared in the course. You can also write an email to swara@nrityanganakalakendra.com for any queries. Video and audio recordings will be available to students who sign up for the online program. There will be 15 live classes.

Evaluation:- Term-end evaluation (conducted online)

- Theory- 10%
- Practical- 40%
- Assignments and Submissions- 50%

Grading System: (percentage)	
O	91-100
A+	81-90
A	71-80
B+	61-70
B	51-60
C	40-50
F	Below 40

Division chart:-

More than or equal to 40 but less than 50
THIRD DIVISION

More than or equal to 50 but less than 60
SECOND DIVISION

More than or equal to 60 but less than 75
FIRST DIVISION

More than or equal to 75 but less than 90
FIRST DIVISION WITH DISTINCTION

90 and above
FIRST DIVISION WITH HONORS

CHAPTER TWELVE

Fine Arts Level 5 (with Presentation)

Course Code: FAL5 (Graduate Diploma)

Eligibility: Successful completion of FAL4B; Class 10th Certificate and Marksheet (or equivalent)

Minimum Duration: 1 year

Maximum Duration: 2 years

*If the learner hasn't completed the course by the end of the given time period, they'll have to re-register to continue.

Registration Fees: Rs. 3000

*Fees after Promotional Discount is Rs. 2700

*Re-registration fees for examination - Rs. 1000

Program Fees: Rs. 4000

*Fees after Promotional Discount is Rs. 3700

Registration and Program Fees: Rs. 7000

*Fees after Promotional Discount is Rs. 6000

Academic Sessions: Flexible Commencement (Validity of 2 years from the date of enrollment)

Examination Sessions: March, June, September, December

*Learner needs to re-register after four examination sessions have been passed. Also, if a learner gives the

examination in a particular session and fails to obtain the minimum marks, they can re-take the examination in the next session (within the four sessions of the enrollment year) for an additional amount of Rs. 1000.

*Once purchased, no amount will be refunded.

*Any malpractice or misconduct from the learner's end would not be tolerated.

Course Coordinator: Prof. Swarnika (swara@nrityanganakalakendra.com)

<u>**Syllabus:-**</u>

The syllabus has been divided into three modules-

<u>FAL5 Module 1</u>

- Surrealism
- Cubism
- Futurism
- Western Art
- Indigenious Art
- Concept of Beauty based on Ancient Scriptures
- Concept of Beauty in the Contemporary world
- Mudra
- Pealism
- Figure Study
- Visual Communication

30 credit hours

<u>FAL5 Module 2</u>

- Portrait - pencil shading
- Portrait - charcoal
- Portrait - water or poster colours
- Portrait - acrylic colours (canvas/ canvas sheet)

- Sculpturing - on a hard surface
- Sculpturing - building from scratch
- Canvas Painting - Nature Study (Acrylic Colours)
- Canvas Painting - Composition (Oil Paint)
- Bibhatsa Rasa Painting
- Adbhuta Rasa Painting

80 credit hours

FAL5 Module 3

- Florence and the Beginning of Renaissance
- Art before 15th Century
- 15th Century Art
- 16th Century Art
- 17th Century Art
- 18th Century Art
- 19th Century Art
- 20th Century Art

50 credit hours

Submission

- Project on Module 1
- Project on Module 3
- Assignment-Paper on Module 3
- Presentation
- Two pencil shading portraits
- Two charcoal portraits
- One water colour portrait
- One poster colour portrait
- Two acrylic colour portraits on canvas

- One Sculptured piece on a pot or uneven surface
- One Sculptured piece on a plain surface (wooden sheet or canvas board)
- One Sculptured piece from scratch
- One Nature Study Canvas Painting with Acrylic Colours
- Two Composition Canvas Painting with Oil Paint
- Bibhatsa Rasa Series
- Adbhuta Rasa Series

Total Credit Hours: 160 hours

Total Credits: 8

Material: The hardcopy of the study material (of all modules) could be availed from Nrityangana Kala Kendra for an additional amount of Rs. 1000. The learners could also buy the study material online. The electronic copy could be purchased from kindle. The relevant links will be shared in the course. You can also write an email to swara@nrityanganakalakendra.com for any queries. Video and audio recordings will be available to students who sign up for the online program. There will be 15 live classes.

Evaluation:- Term-end evaluation (conducted online)

- Theory- 10%
- Practical- 40%
- Assignments and Submissions- 50%

Grading System: (percentage)	
O	91-100
A+	81-90
A	71-80
B+	61-70
B	51-60
C	40-50
F	Below 40

Division chart:-

More than or equal to 40 but less than 50
THIRD DIVISION

More than or equal to 50 but less than 60
SECOND DIVISION

More than or equal to 60 but less than 75
FIRST DIVISION

More than or equal to 75 but less than 90
FIRST DIVISION WITH DISTINCTION

90 and above
FIRST DIVISION WITH HONORS

CHAPTER THIRTEEN

Post-Graduate diploma in Fine Arts

Course Code: PGDFA

Eligibility: Successful completion of FAL5; Class 12th Certificate and Marksheet (or equivalent)

Minimum Duration: 1 year

Maximum Duration: 3 years

*If the learner hasn't completed the course by the end of the given time period, they'll have to re-register to continue.

Registration Fees: Rs. 4500

*Fees after Promotional Discount is Rs. 4000

*Re-registration fees for examination - Rs. 1000

Program Fees: Rs. 6000

*Fees after Promotional Discount is Rs. 5500

Registration and Program Fees: Rs. 10,500

*Fees after Promotional Discount is Rs. 9000

Academic Sessions: Flexible Commencement (Validity of 3 years from the date of enrollment)

Examination Sessions: March, June, September, December

*Learner needs to re-register after four examination sessions have been passed. Also, if a learner gives the

examination in a particular session and fails to obtain the minimum marks, they can re-take the examination in the next session (within the four sessions of the enrollment year) for an additional amount of Rs. 1000.

*Once purchased, no amount will be refunded.

*Any malpractice or misconduct from the learner's end would not be tolerated.

Course Coordinator: Prof. Swarnika (swara@nrityanganakalakendra.com)

<u>Syllabus:-</u>

The syllabus has been divided into three modules-

<u>PGDFA Module 1</u>

* Drawing and Painting
* History of Indian Architecture
* History of Indian Painting and Sculpture
* Principles and Sources of Art

40 credit hours

<u>PGDFA Module 2</u>

* History of Western Art from early times to 1400 AD
* History of Western Art from 1400 AD to 1850 AD
* History of Modern Movements in Art in India
* History of Modern Movements in Art in Europe and USA

50 credit hours

<u>PGDFA Module 3</u>

* Picture Composition

- Still Lfe
- Natural Landscape
- Charcoal Painting
- Oil Painting
- Acrylic Painting
- Pencil Shading
- Illustrations
- Designing (posters, covers, freehand, floral, geometric, etc)
- Modern Art
- Abstract Art
- Folk Art
- Antique Study
- Portrait Painting
- Canvas Painting
- Shanta Rasa Painting

100 credit hours

PGDFA Module 4

- Research Paper 1
- Research Paper 2
- Project 1 (subjective)
- Project 2 (allotted)
- Shanta Rasa Series
- Navras Series (9 clippings)

50 credit hours

Submission

- Essays on all units of Module 1

- Essays on all units of Module 2
- Two submissions of each topic in Module 3

Total Credit Hours: 240 hours

Total Credits: 12

Material: The hardcopy of the study material (of all modules) could be availed from Nrityangana Kala Kendra for an additional amount of Rs. 1000. The learners could also buy the study material online. The electronic copy could be purchased from kindle. The relevant links will be shared in the course. You can also write an email to swara@nrityanganakalakendra.com for any queries. Video and audio recordings will be available to students who sign up for the online program. There will be 15 live classes.

Evaluation:- Term-end evaluation (conducted online)

- Theory- 10%
- Practical- 40%
- Assignments and Submissions- 50%

Grading System: (percentage)	
O	91-100
A+	81-90
A	71-80
B+	61-70
B	51-60
C	40-50
F	Below 40

Division chart:-

More than or equal to 40 but less than 50
THIRD DIVISION

More than or equal to 50 but less than 60
SECOND DIVISION

More than or equal to 60 but less than 75
FIRST DIVISION

More than or equal to 75 but less than 90
FIRST DIVISION WITH DISTINCTION

90 and above
FIRST DIVISION WITH HONORS

www.ingramcontent.com/pod-product-compliance
Lightning Source LLC
Chambersburg PA
CBHW031421160726
47993CB00003B/1338